Performing Artist

CLAUDE DEBUSSY
Piano Works
Edited by Joseph Banowetz

This volume is for Pamela Paul, great Debussy interpreter and loyal friend.

Director of Keyboard Publications: GAIL LEW
Project Manager: DALE TUCKER
Art Design: LISA GREENE MANE

ONTENTS

$\mathscr{A}$BOUT THE EDITOR

JOSEPH BANOWETZ has been described in *Fanfare Record Review* (United States) as "a giant among keyboard artists of our time" and by *Russia's News* (Moscow) as "a magnificent virtuoso." He has been heard as recitalist and orchestral soloist on five continents, with guest appearances in recent seasons with such orchestras as the St. Petersburg (formerly the Leningrad) Philharmonic, the New Zealand Symphony (in a twelve-concert national tour), the Prague Radio Symphony, the Moscow State Symphony, the Belarus National Philharmonic of Minsk, the Hong Kong Philharmonic, the Shanghai Symphony, and the Beijing Central Philharmonic.

Banowetz has received international critical acclaim for his series of compact disc recordings for the Marco Polo, Naxos, and Altarus labels. His world-premiere recording of Balakirev works received a German Music Critics' outstanding record of the year award, and his world-premiere recording of Anton Rubinstein's Concertos Nos. 1 and 2 received a similar citation from *Fanfare Record Review* (U.S.). He has recorded twenty-two compact discs including concertos of Tchaikovsky's, Liszt's, and d'Albert's and the world-premiere recordings of all eight of the Anton Rubinstein works for piano and orchestra. Banowetz has recorded with the Moscow Symphony, Prague Radio Symphony, the Czecho-Slovak State Philharmonic, the Budapest Symphony, the Beijing Central Opera Orchestra, and the Hong Kong Philharmonic.

A graduate with a First Prize from the Vienna Academy for Music and Dramatic Arts, Banowetz also studied with Carl Friedberg (a pupil of Clara Schumann's) and Gÿorgy Sándor (a pupil of Béla Bartók's). In addition to his performance and recording activities, he has given lectures and master classes at such schools as the Juilliard in New York City, the St. Petersburg Conservatory, the Royal College of Music in London, the Chopin Academy of Warsaw, the Beijing Central Conservatory, the Shanghai Conservatory, and the Hong Kong Academy for the Performing Arts.

Banowetz has been invited to serve on many international piano competition juries, these having included the Gina Bachauer International Piano Competition (United States), the 2001 World Piano Competition (United States), the Arthur Rubinstein International Piano Master Competition (Israel), the Scottish International Piano Competition (Glasgow), and the PTNA Young Artists Competition (Japan). His award-winning book *The Pianist's Guide to Pedaling* has been printed in five languages. In 1992 Banowetz was presented with the Liszt Medal by the Hungarian Liszt Society in Budapest. Mr. Banowetz is a Steinway artist.

PERFORMANCE NOTES

Page d'album

This work, which was untitled by Debussy, was written in 1915, to be sold for the benefit of a war relief organization named Le Vêtement du blessé (The Clothing of the Wounded). The music has the character of a slow waltz.

Measures 7 and 8: Push ahead the tempo slightly until the beginning of measure 9, where there is a resumption of the original tempo. Note that in measures 11 and 12, Debussy does not indicate a parallel quickening of the tempo.

Measures 19–22: Show a distinction between the *pianissimo* here and the *piano* found at the beginning when this same theme appears.

Measures 24–27: Carefully follow the sudden drops of dynamics back to *piano*.

Measures 27–30: The *rubato* indicates a freedom in the rhythm. Hold together these measures as a four-bar phrase, perhaps starting a little slower, speeding up, and then slowing back down at the end of the phrase in measure 30.

Measures 37–38: Keep this measure in tempo, as a sort of elegant "throw-away" ending.

Le petit nègre

This humorous little piece in ragtime style was written for Théodore Lack's piano method and then published in 1909 by Alphonse Leduc, who again brought it out in 1934 in an expanded version not originally by Debussy. Its style is related to the "Golliwogg's Cake Walk" from the *Children's Corner Suite* and can be used as an introduction to it. A cake walk is an elaborate step or strutting dance that was originally performed by Negroes in the American South competing for the prize of a cake.

Throughout this piece, a clear differentiation of touches is extremely important. Relatively little pedal should be used so as to project the sharp, incisive touches and rhythms. Only in measures 16–25 and 29–33, where the outlines of the music become more rounded, can some more pedal be used.

Measures 1–3, 5–7, etc.: Carefully show the slurring. Even a short slur over two sixteenths, as in measures 3 and 7, should be shown.

Measures 3–12: Differences in touches should be clear to the listener. For instance, in measures 3–7 the left hand is given a *portato* touch, in measure 8 there are two slurs in the left hand, and in measures 9–12 the left hand has a *staccato* touch.

Arabesque No. 1

Debussy's two arabesques were first published in 1891 but actually date from 1888. The style cannot yet be termed "impressionistic." The composer himself later perhaps implied the meaning of the titles when he spoke of Bach's "adorable arabesques."

Throughout the piece, lightly stress the lowest notes in each left-hand figuration, these usually falling on the first and third beats.

Measures 7, 9, 10, and 11: When the pedal is changed on each second beat, hold the first two eighths of the left hand long enough to sustain them as a new pedal is taken. This "finger pedaling" will enable the bass to be maintained in an unbroken line.

Measure 39: Notice the *tempo rubato* indication, therefore giving you the freedom to "let go" and play in an improvisatory manner.

Measures 47–49: Note the differences in phrasing and slurring in both the left and right hands.

Measures 89–94: Carefully hold over, as well as lightly emphasize, the half notes in the left hand.

Measures 99–107: Play from measure 99 to the end in *tempo,* as if this is the curtain coming down on an elegant play or opera.

Arabesque No. 2

Measures 1–7, and later similar passages: It is important that the triplet sixteenth-eighth note figures be extremely precise rhythmically. A good way to practice is to tap a rapid eighth-note rhythm with the left hand while playing the right-hand notes. Start with a lower wrist as you begin each triplet, and then lift slightly as you reach the eighth note. This will keep your arm and hand from getting tense and, more important, will shape each group properly. Throughout this entire piece, use very little pedal.

Measures 38–40: Do not be tempted to use pedal to connect the left hand since this will blur the *staccato* notes in the right hand.

Measures 82–89: This is the only area requiring longer stretches of pedal. In later works in particular, Debussy often indicates such stretches of pedal by writing longer notes, often in the bass, that cannot be held by the fingers alone.

Rêverie

The exact date of composition of this early work is unknown, although Debussy sold it, along with a group of other early works, to the Choudens publishing company in 1891. Fromont finally published it in 1905, much to Debussy's chagrin, who by that time was composing works of much greater musical maturity. Nonetheless, it has proven to be one of his most popular works for piano largely because of the elegant melody set against a Chopinesque texture.

Measures 1–8: When the pedal is changed because of the melody, hold over as many notes in the left hand as you can with the fingers. For instance, in measures 4–5, play as follows:

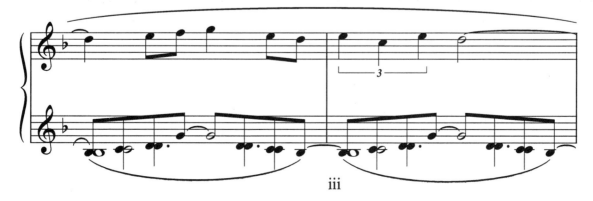

Measures 23–26: On many pianos, you will not need a pedal change on the downbeat of measure 25, assuming you make a good, steady *crescendo*. Experiment and listen carefully to yourself!

Measures 69–70: Bring out the melody clearly in the lower quarter notes of the left hand.

Measures 76–81: This is a wonderful use by Debussy of the venerable three-hand effect, first used extensively and with great brilliance by Liszt and Sigismond Thalberg. Here, try to shape the overall melody as well as its first occurence in the opening bars of the piece.

Prélude, from *Suite bergamasque*

The *Suite bergamasque* was written around 1889 and then appeared in 1905 in a revised version published by Fromont. The word *bergamasque* probably had its origins in the Bergamo region of northern Italy. It is from this region that a dance called bergamasca came and that the cast of characters from the antique Italian *Comedia dell'Arte* can be traced. The entire *Suite bergamasque* can also be regarded as a transformation of the older Baroque suite, with the "Prélude" serving as a brilliant improvisatory first movement and the "Clair de lune" as the slower dance movement.

One of the difficulties found in this lovely work is the occurence of large unbroken left-hand chords, which demand a stretch of a tenth. In many cases, redistribution will solve this problem if the performer is not fortunate enough to have such a large hand. Following are possible solutions, additional to the redistributions already indicated in the musical text in measures 10, 18, 22, 38, and 68.

Measure 1: By the indication *tempo rubato*, Debussy is asking for a certain freedom and flexibility in the rhythm. For instance, in measures 1 and 2, the performer could hold the half-note chord slightly longer, start the sixteenth notes slower, then speed up, and finally reach a stable tempo in the first half of measures 3 and 4. A slight pushing of the tempo to the downbeat in the second half of measures 3 and 4 would offset the more strict tempo of the first half of each of these measures. (This gives only a very rough idea of how *tempo rubato* could be used here!)

Measure 3: The following redistribution is possible. Note that the whole-note A in the left hand must be silently re-depressed again with the left hand before the pedal is changed on the third beat. If this is used, a slightly different pedaling is necessary.

Measures 5–6: Here Debussy writes in a real four-part, almost fugal, style. Keep a good legato with the fingers so as to not lose the tied and held notes in each part when the pedal is changed. Do some practicing without pedal.

Measure 19: Ideally the low whole-note F on the downbeat should be heard through the entire measure. Underplay slightly the D-B♭ and B♭-G thirds in the right hand so as to more easily maintain the basic F major harmony. Another solution (favored by the editor) is to use the following redistribution as a form of finger pedaling. Note the pedaling.

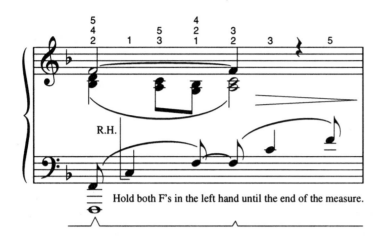

Measures 21, 24, and similar later places: Smaller hands should roll the left-hand chords slightly before the beat, carefully catching the lowest notes in each change of pedal.

Measures 26–29: Problems with these large left-hand stretches can be solved with the following redistributions:

Measures 30–31: As in measures 5 and 6, keep a good finger *legato* so that each part remains connected. See also measures 44–51. Do some practicing without pedal.

Measure 88: Note that Debussy's accent is placed under the A, which is the last note of the melody. Playing the chord using 5-3 instead of 5-4 will help facilitate this difficult voicing.

Clair de lune, from *Suite bergamasque*

Do not sentimentalize this delicately shimmering work with exaggerated *rubatos* and other cheap effects, but rather try to play with an expressive simplicity and elegance.

Measures 5–8: The downbeats should not be accented so that the tied notes of the melody can clearly sound through from the measure before.

Measures 10–14: These measures are good examples of how Debussy often indicates how he wishes the pedaling by the use of long notes. Since each dotted half note on each downbeat must be carried through, do not change the pedal until the next measure. Only in measure 14 can a possible half pedal change be taken, which incidentally may not be necessary on all pianos, especially when playing in a larger hall.

Measure 15: The *tempo rubato* marking indicates there should be flexibility of the rhythm. For example, perhaps pause slightly on the first chord, then push ahead until the second half of measure 16, and then relax the tempo.

Measures 19–25: Begin measure 19 still at a *pianissimo,* and then carry the *crescendo* to the downbeat of measure 25. Calculate your rate of *crescendo* carefully, being approximately *piano* at the start of measure 21, *mezzo piano* at the start of measure 23, and finally a non-percussive *forte* in measure 25. A common mistake in a long *crescendo* is to get too loud too soon. Knowing approximately where you want to be in dynamic levels, somewhat like following road signs, is a helpful means of conquering this bad habit.

Measures 25–26: Make each roll not only slower than the one before, but also softer. Again, use "road signs," the first roll being *forte,* the next *mezzo forte,* the next *mezzo piano,* and the last *piano.* This sets the stage for the *pianissimo* of measure 27.

Measures 27–42: Follow the dynamics exactly. The climax of this entire section, which is only a *forte,* comes in measure 41. When you memorize, learn not only the notes but the exact dynamics as well. Know what they are at any given moment, and not just as a vague "now I get louder" or "now I get softer"!

Measure 30: Lightly bring out, like an echo, the G-F-D♭-D♭-B♭ answer in the middle voice.

Measure 43: Notice that from here to the end of the piece, the dynamics should never be above a *pianissimo* and will be *pianississimo* for part of the time.

Measures 63–65: Avoid making a *crescendo* in order to set the mood better for the *morendo* (dying away) indication in measure 66.

Selections from *Children's Corner Suite*

Debussy's *Children's Corner Suite* was composed between 1906 and 1908. He dedicated it to his daughter, Claude-Emma, with the following inscription: "To my dear little Chouchou with her father's apologies for what is to follow." Debussy's daughter outlived her father by only one year, dying in 1919 at the age of fourteen. These lovely works continue to captivate listeners and performers of all ages.

Dr. Gradus ad Parnassum

Debussy is perhaps suggesting a child's frustrating struggles with exercises from Clementi's *Gradus ad Parnassum.* Debussy, perhaps with tongue in cheek, termed this piece "a kind of progressive hygienic, gymnastic exercise to be played every morning."

Measures 3–6: Show a clear difference in touches between the eighth-note *staccato* top notes in measures 3 and 4 and the *legato* quarter notes in measures 5 and 6.

Measures 67 and 69: The editor takes the A's with the right hand.

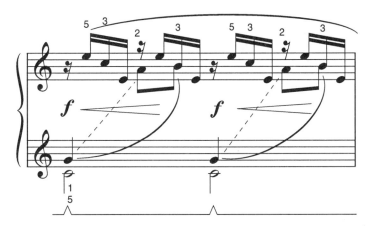

Serenade for the Doll

This piece was first published separately in 1906 and is a tribute to one of his daughter's favorite dolls.

It is quite possible to play this piece entirely without damper pedal until reaching Debussy's indication for it in measures 121–123.

Measures 1–13: Keep the E-Bs uniformly even in dynamics, except for the sudden *forte* in measure 8. Do not let them follow the dynamics in the melody.

Measure 13: Taking the last E-B with the right hand will help ensure that there is no *crescendo* or accent before the sudden *forte* in measure 14.

Measure 66–105: Pay close attention to which notes are rolled. For instance, in measures 83–84 there are rolls in the left hand, in measures 86–89 no rolls, and in measures 90–92 rolls in both hands.

Measures 107–114: Carefully observe the sudden shifts of dynamics in the right hand.

Measures 115–118: Try to make these measures sound as if you would play them as follows:

The Little Shepherd

This is a rather melancholy picture of a toy shepherd. Throughout, the most precise dynamics are called for. There are lovely echo effects, for instance in measures 3 and 4 and measures 24 and 25. Debussy at times uses dynamics between dynamics, as in measures 8–10, where he begins *piano,* goes to *più piano* (more soft), and then goes to *pianissimo* in the right hand and *pianississimo* in the left hand. Depending on the instrument you play, try to use the *una corda* only for *pianissimo* and softer.

Measure 24: This is the dynamic climax of the entire piece. Only in measure 3 does Debussy give another *mezzo forte* indication, everywhere else indicating *piano* or below.

Measures 27–30: In measure 27 start *pianissimo,* and then go down to *pianississimo.* In measure 28 start *piano,* and then drop to a *pianissimo* at the beginning of measure 29. Keep getting softer until you reach the *pianississimo* in measure 30.

Golliwogg's Cake Walk

In Europe during the early 1900s, a little black doll named Golliwogg was enormously popular. In style, this piece is related, through its use of minstrel rhythms, to "Le petit nègre," also included in this collection.

Measures 1–4: Make distinctions between the various types of accents, such as the following:

> A A

Measures 6–15: Keep the left hand uniformly *piano* and *staccato.*

Measures 10–11, 18–19, and 98–99: Possibly redistribute these measures as follows:

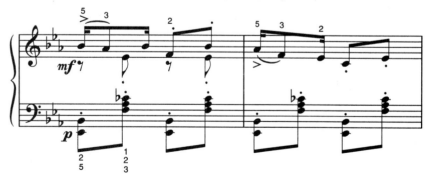

Measures 16–17: Take the *crescendo* up to a strong *fortissimo,* and then immediately drop back to a *forte* on the downbeat of measure 18.

Measures 27, 35, 107, 115: Most performers hold the pedal through each of these measures in order to hold the D-F half notes. Another solution is possible that allows the eighth notes to still sound *staccato* and unpedaled.

Measure 29: This measure can also be redistributed as follows:

Measure 33: If pedal is used on the last eighth note, it should only be for accenting. Release it quickly; otherwise, a carry-over of sound into the next *piano* will result. On a large concert instrument, this pedaling may be unnecessary.

Measures 47–59: All the grace notes should be played very rapidly and before each beat. Use a quick upward flip of the wrist, while pulling in with the fingers playing the chords. In measures 49 and 57, Debussy's marking (see example) is somewhat ambiguous in meaning. A small rubato as well as a slight expressive stressing of the grace note may be what is intended.

Measures 61–63 and 65–67: Debussy detested the music of Wagner. Here he makes fun of the opening of Wagner's opera *Tristan and Isolde*.

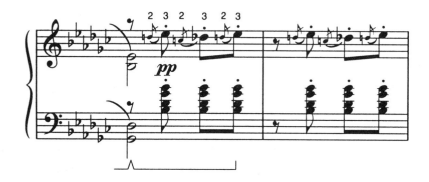

Lento e languido
Langsam und schmachtend

The opening to Wagner's *Prelude* to his opera *Tristan and Isolde*

Measures 67 and 68: These measures can be redistributed as follows to make it easier to play the grace notes in a rapid, clear manner. See also measure 78.

Measures 90–92: Do not gradually get faster in measures 90–91; then make the return to tempo one in measure 92 sudden and unexpected.

La fille aux cheveux de lin (from *Préludes*, Bk. 1)

This portrait of "The Girl with the Flaxen Hair" remains one of Debussy's most popular works for the piano. Play it with simplicity and an unexaggerated expressiveness.

Measures 2–3: Do not accent the downbeat of measure 3; be careful to make clear the small *decrescendo* at the end of measure 2. This will help prevent any feeling of rhythmic squareness.

Measure 12: Roll the right hand on, not before, the beat so as to avoid a break in the melody and to be able to catch all the notes in the pedal.

Measure 13: When the pedal is partially cleared on the first beat, be sure to hold the right hand G♭ with the fifth finger to avoid a break in the melody. Another way of pedaling this is as follows:

If you use this pedaling, hold only the lowest G♭ in the left hand when you change the pedal on the high G♭ in the right hand.

Measure 31: In the left hand, first play the lowest E♭-B♭ slightly before the beat and then the top G♭-B♭-E♭ with the notes in the right hand. Slightly hold back the last two sixteenths in measure 30 to help make this necessary delay musically convincing.

Measures 37–38: Imagine the sound of the two broken octaves as the sound of a harp being plucked.

ℬIOGRAPHY OF CLAUDE DEBUSSY

Claude Debussy's place in musical history as one of France's greatest composers remains secure. Born August 22, 1862, near Paris in St.-Germain-en-Laye, his father was proprietor of a china shop. Debussy had early piano lessons with Mme. Mauté de Fleurville, the mother-in-law of the French poet Paul Verlaine, and then at the age of eleven was admitted to the Paris Conservatoire. Debussy proved to be an excellent student, although he was not popular with either the faculty or his classmates because of his uncommunicative and surly manner. He sarcastically termed César Franck, one of his teachers, a modulating machine, and when asked by another instructor what rules he followed, answered back, "My own pleasure." Nonetheless, Debussy was awarded first prizes in both solfège and practical harmony shortly before his graduation.

Debussy spent 1881 and 1882 in the employment of Mme. Nadezhda von Meck, Tchaikovsky's patroness. His duties included acting as the household's piano teacher and resident performer during the von Meck family's travel's to Switzerland, Italy, and Russia. Mme. von Meck, in a letter to Tchaikovsky, described Debussy as "Parisian from tip to toe, a typical gamin, very witty and an excellent mimic." He was fired when he unsuccessfully proposed marriage to von Meck's eldest daughter, Sonia.

In 1884, after further composition studies at the Conservatoire, Debussy was awarded a coveted Prix de Rome, which enabled him to live for three years at government expense at the Villa Medici in Rome. During this time, he was expected to compose as well as submit some of his work each year to the authorities in Paris for evaluation. At the end of the first year, it was reported that "at present M. Debussy seems to be afflicted with a desire to compose music that is bizarre, incomprehensible, and impossible to execute." Debussy despised Italy and all that was Italian, and in the spring of 1887 he decided to return to Paris before completing his residency. His days as a student were over.

Although Debussy was briefly captivated by the music of Richard Wagner, soon he developed a bitter hatred of all Wagnerisms and consequently championed the French ideals of conciseness and clarity. These ideals are increasingly reflected in his music. Debussy also encountered both the music of the Russian Nationalists, as well as music of the Far East, at the 1889 Exposition held in Paris. These musical styles, too, would prove to be exotic influences on his work. Most important, during the 1890s, Debussy became personally acquainted with the leading impressionistic painters and symbolist poets of the day.

By this time, Debussy's personality had become complex and reserved and was pervaded by an unpleasantly aggressive egoism that made him appear cold and sarcastic to most people. He was short and plump with a pale complexion and a huge forehead protruding over penetrating, heavily lidded eyes. Since his return from Rome in 1887, he had been living with Gabrielle Duport. She left him after having shot herself following an argument. A marriage followed two years later to Rosalie Texier, a dressmaker. In 1904 Debussy left her, and she, too, shot herself, but recovered. Debussy finally found some domestic happiness with Emma Bardac, whom he married in 1908. Emma was relatively well-off, having been married to a wealthy banker. Debussy and Emma had one daughter, Chouchou, who tragically died at the age of fourteen, just a year after Debussy's own death.

The final fifteen years of Debussy's life were spent primarily in Paris, although he occasionally paid visits to such cities as Budapest, Vienna, Moscow, Amsterdam, and Rome to conduct his own works. It was during this period that he wrote the caustic series of music reviews and articles that earned him the reputation as one of the day's most perceptive critics. By the summer of 1909, Debussy began to feel symptoms of the cancer that would bring him an agonizing death on March 25, 1918, as the Germans were bombarding Paris. At the end, he wrote tragically about his "life of waiting—my waiting-room existence, I might call it—for I am a poor traveller waiting for a train that will never come any more."

EBUSSY AND THE PIANO

Debussy's manner of playing was, from all accounts, highly unique. When the Italian composer Alfredo Casella heard Debussy play, he wrote:

> He played without a real and proper virtuosity in the bravura sense, but still possessed an inimitable art of touch and pedaling. He sometimes seemed to play directly on the strings, without passing through the mechanism of the piano, so vaporous and usubstantial was his sonority . . . . His rhythm was perfect, and the two hands always played precisely together. Even in the predominantly harmonic music he wrote, every melodic and rhythmic accent had its just value.

Maurice Dumesnil, who played for Debussy, wrote:

> I noticed that at times the position of his fingers, particularly in soft chord passages, was almost flat. He seemed to caress the keys by rubbing them gently downward in an oblique motion instead of pushing them down in a straight line.

Another Debussy pupil, the famous French pianist and pedagogue Marguerite Long, observed:

> He played almost always in half shades, but with a full and intense sonority that had not harshness in the attack . . . . The scale of his nuances went from *pianississimo* to *forte* without ever arriving at immoderate sonorities.

Although Debussy in 1904 recorded a few accompaniments for Mary Garden, the creator of his first operatic *Mélisande,* there are no other sound recordings by him. He did make a number of piano rolls for the Welte Company, but although they are of undeniable interest, these remain unreliable in many respects. Pianists from the time, some of whom played for Debussy, recorded Debussy's music. These include Alfred Cortot (1877–1962), Marguerite Long (1874–1966), George Copeland (1882–1971), E. Robert Schmitz (1889–1949), Harold Bauer (1873–1951), Daniel Ericourt (1903-1998), Ricardo Viñes (1875–1943), Robert Casadesus (1899–1972), and Guiomar Novaës (1896–1979). Walter Gieseking (1895–1956), who did not personally come in contact with Debussy, is regarded by many as the finest interpreter of his music in the twentieth century. Perhaps the best way someone today can come in contact with Debussy's pianistic style is to study some of the recordings of these often very diverse interpreters.

$\mathscr{S}$UGGESTIONS FOR FURTHER READING

Debussy, Claude. "Monsieur Croche," in *Three Classics in the Aesthetics of Music*. New York: Dover Publications, 1962. (A collection of Debussy's reviews and articles on music, which is both indispensable and entertaining.)

Dumesnil, Maurice. *How to Play and Teach Debussy*. New York: Schroeder and Gunther, Inc., 1932. (This contains important suggestions on how to play Debussy's piano music by a former Debussy student.)

Lockspeiser, Edward. *Debussy: His Life and Mind*. 2 vols. London: Cassell, 1962 and 1965. (This still remains an important biography for anyone studying Debussy's life and music.)

Schmitz, E. Robert. *The Piano Works of Claude Debussy*. New York: Dover, 1966. (Schmitz's book, written by someone who played extensively for the composer, has long remained one of the most valuable books on Debussy's piano music.)

Thompson, Oscar. *Debussy: Man and Artist*. New York: Dover, 1967. (This is the first American biography of Debussy. It contains not only a fine biography of the composer, but also perceptive discussions of his individual works.)

Vallas, Léon. *Claude Debussy: His Life and Works*. New York: Dover, 1973. (This is a famous biography by a personal acquaintance of the composer's.)

Deuxième Arabesque, Autograph (first page) (Bibliothèque Nationale, Paris)

PAGE D'ALBUM
Album Leaf

CLAUDE DEBUSSY
Edited by Joseph Banowetz

* Debussy gives no tempo indication or title. The Editor suggests moderato, ♩=120-126.

Page d'Album - 2 - 1

ELM00044

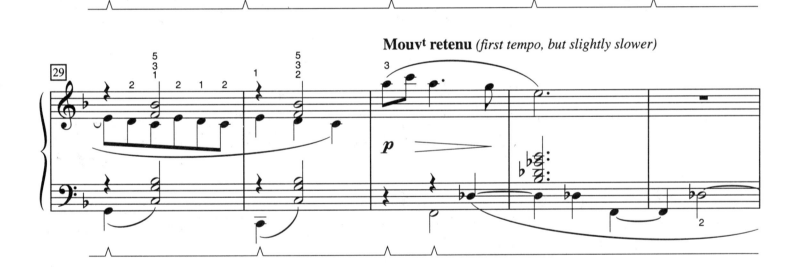

LE PETIT NÈGRE
(Cake Walk)

CLAUDE DEBUSSY
Edited by Joseph Banowetz

Allegro giusto (♩ = 126–132)*

f très rhthmé
(very rhythmical)

f marcato

mf e dim.

f

mf

dim.

un peu retenu
(a little holding back)

cresc. molto

f

mf

* Debussy gave no metronome indication.

Le Petit Nègre - 3 - 1
ELM00044

doux et expressif
(sweet and expressive)

retenu *(hold back)*

6

TWO ARABESQUES

Arabesque I

CLAUDE DEBUSSY
Edited by Joseph Banowetz

Andantino con moto (♩ = 126–132)*

* Debussy gave no metronome indication.

8

Arabesque I - 6 - 4
ELM00044

Arabesque II

CLAUDE DEBUSSY
Edited by Joseph Banowetz

Allegretto scherzando (♩ = 116–120)*

p et très léger (and very light)

dim.

pp

pp

sf

---

* Debussy gave no metronome indication.

Arabesque II - 7 - 1

ELM00044

14

16

18

RÊVERIE

CLAUDE DEBUSSY
Edited by Joseph Banowetz

(without dragging)
Andantino sans lenteur (♩ = 100–104)*

(very sweet and very expressive)
très doux et très expressif

pp

p

meno ***p***

mf

* Debussy gave no metronome indication.

22

PRÉLUDE

(from *Suite bergamasque*)

CLAUDE DEBUSSY
Edited by Joseph Banowetz

* See the notes for performance and interpretation for a possible solution for more easily playing the large chords in the left hand in bars 26-29.

28

Prélude (from *Suite bergamasque*) - 6 - 5

ELM00044

CLAIR DE LUNE

Moonlight
(from *Suite bergamasque*)

CLAUDE DEBUSSY
Edited by Joseph Banowetz

(very expressive)
Andante très expressif (♩. = 56–58)*

*Debussy gave no metronome indication.

Clair de Lune
(from *Suite bergamasque*) - 7 - 1
ELM00044

Tempo rubato

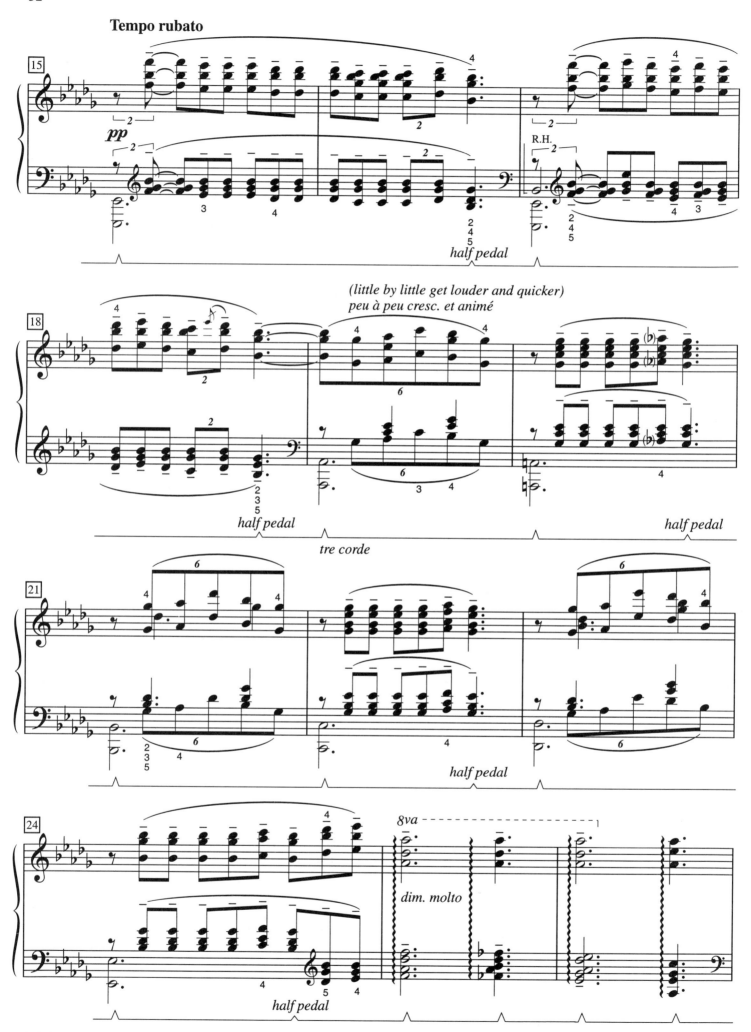

(little by little get louder and quicker)
peu à peu cresc. et animé

half pedal

tre corde

half pedal

half pedal

half pedal

8va

dim. molto

half pedal

*An effective distribution is to take the bottom three notes with the left hand, the next four notes with right hand, and the top A flat with the left hand crossed over.

DOCTOR GRADUS AD PARNASSUM

(from *Children's Corner*)

CLAUDE DEBUSSY
Edited by Joseph Banowetz

Modérément animé *(moderately lively)* (♩ = 126–132)*

p égal et sans sécheresse
(even and without dryness)

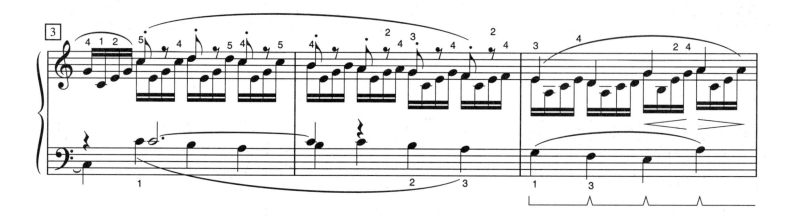

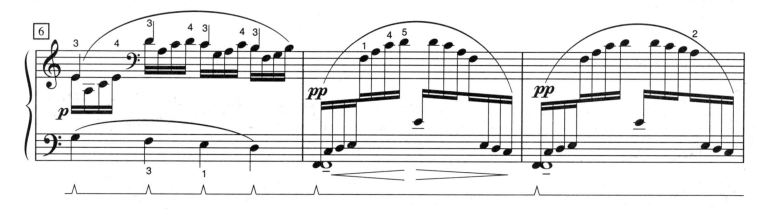

* Debussy gave no metronome indication.

Doctor Gradus ad Parnassum
(from *Children's Corner*) - 5 - 1

ELM00044

Doctor Gradus ad Parnassum (from *Children's Corner*) - 5 - 2

ELM00044

En animant peu à peu (little by little get faster)

Doctor Gradus ad Parnassum (from *Children's Corner*) - 5 - 4

ELM00044

Très animé (very lively)

SERENADE OF THE DOLL

(from *Children's Corner*)

CLAUDE DEBUSSY
Edited by Joseph Banowetz

Allegretto ma non troppo (♩ = 116–120)*

Très léger et gracieux (very light and graceful)

la m.g. un peu en dehors
(emphasize a little the left hand)

(emphasize a little the right hand)
la m.d. un peu en dehors

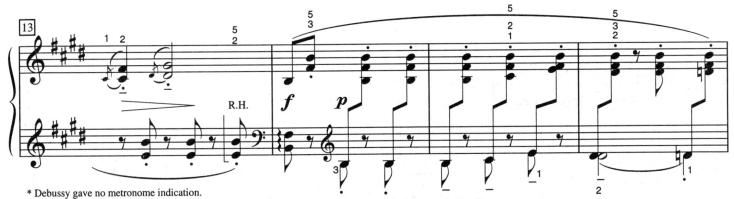

* Debussy gave no metronome indication.

** *Il faudra mettre la pédale sourde pendant toute la durée de ce morceau, même aux endroits marqués d'un f.*
(One must use the soft pedal through the whole duration of this piece, even at places marked with an *f.*)

Serenade of the Doll
(from *Children's Corner*) - 6 - 1

ELM00044

44

poco a poco cresc.

Un peu retenu (a little holding back)

(slow down)
Cédez

a tempo

(expressive)
expressif

(becoming a little more lively)
En animant un peu

Serenade of the Doll (from *Children's Corner*) - 6 - 3

ELM00044

Serenade of the Doll (from *Children's Corner*) - 6 - 5

ELM00044

48

* Debussy's original indication for the damper pedal is given here. Because of the extreme delicacy and transparency of the music's texture, the Editor prefers to play the entire piece up to this point without any damper pedal whatsoever.

Serenade of the Doll (from *Children's Corner*) - 6 - 6

ELM00044

Claude Debussy while at the Conservatoire (about 1874)

Claude Debussy (about 1895)

THE LITTLE SHEPHERD

(from *Children's Corner*)

CLAUDE DEBUSSY
Edited by Joseph Banowetz

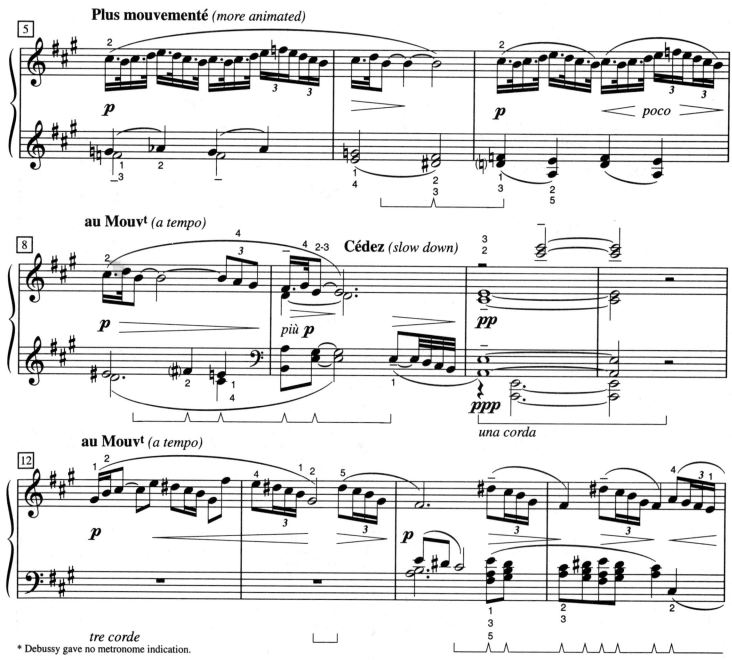

* Debussy gave no metronome indication.

The Little Shepherd
(from *Children's Corner*) - 2 - 1

ELM00044

GOLLIWOGG'S CAKE-WALK

(from *Children's Corner*)

CLAUDE DEBUSSY
Edited by Joseph Banowetz

Allegro giusto (♩ = 112–116)*

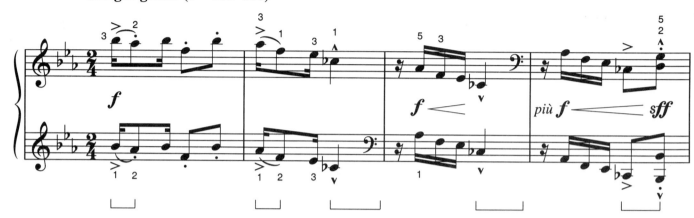

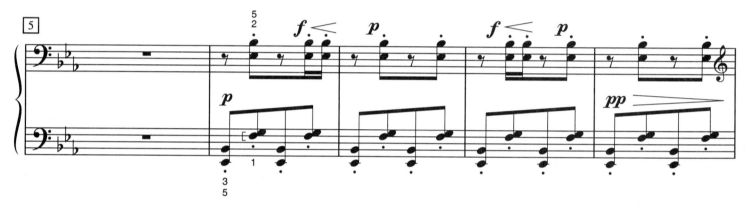

très net et très sec (very clear and very crisp)

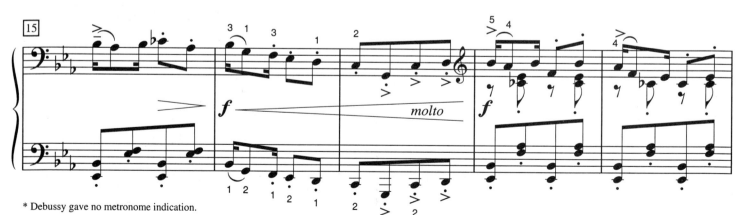

* Debussy gave no metronome indication.

Golliwogg's Cake-Walk - 6 - 1
ELM00044

* An alternate redistribution, which is used by the Editor, is given in the notes for performance and interpretation. See similar places in bars 37, 109, and 117.

Golliwogg's Cake-Walk - 6 - 2
ELM00044

Un peu moins vite *(a little less rapid)*

Cédez *(slow down)*
avec une grande émotion
(with much emotion)

a tempo

Cédez *(slow down)*

* A use of the sostenuto pedal can be very useful in bars 84-86 and 88-89, both to sustain clearly the held chords, while allowing the B flat - A flat - B flat motive above to be heard with an unblurred, distinct *staccato* touch.

LA FILLE AUX CHEVEUX DE LIN
The Girl with the Flaxen Hair
(from *Préludes*, Book I)

CLAUDE DEBUSSY
Edited by Joseph Banowetz

* This metronome indication was given by Debussy.

Un peu animé *(a little more lively)*

Cédez *(slow down)*

au Mouv^t *(resume tempo)*
sans lourdeur (without heaviness)

una corda

Claude Debussy (about 1900)

La fille aux cheveux de lin (The Girl With the Flaxen Hair), measures 1–32

Debussy outside his home (about 1910)

Debussy at Pourville (September 1904)

Debussy, by Jacques-Émile Blanche (1903)